50 Cooking Delicious Brunch Recipes

By: Kelly Johnson

Table of Contents

- Classic Eggs Benedict
- Avocado Toast with Poached Egg
- French Toast Casserole
- Spinach and Feta Quiche
- Smoked Salmon Bagels
- Banana Pancakes with Maple Syrup
- Shakshuka (Poached Eggs in Tomato Sauce)
- Breakfast Burritos
- Brioche French Toast
- Veggie Omelette with Goat Cheese
- Spinach and Mushroom Frittata
- Sweet Potato Hash
- Lemon Ricotta Pancakes
- Egg and Avocado Breakfast Sandwich
- Croissant Breakfast Sandwich
- Chia Pudding with Mixed Berries
- Buttermilk Waffles with Whipped Cream
- Roasted Tomato and Herb Salad
- Blueberry Muffins
- Baked Eggs with Spinach and Bacon
- Smoothie Bowls with Fresh Toppings
- Cucumber and Cream Cheese Sandwiches
- Grilled Cheese and Tomato Soup
- Chicken and Waffle Sliders
- Smashed Avocado and Toast with Poached Eggs
- Greek Yogurt Parfait with Granola
- Sweet Corn Fritters
- Salmon Croquettes with Dill Sauce
- Mimosas with Fresh Orange Juice
- Sourdough Pancakes
- Caprese Salad with Fresh Mozzarella
- Zucchini Fritters with Lemon Aioli
- Breakfast Tacos with Salsa Verde
- Roasted Vegetable Tart
- Bacon, Egg, and Cheese Croissant

- Stuffed Bell Peppers with Quinoa and Eggs
- Lemon Poppy Seed Muffins
- Quinoa Salad with Roasted Veggies
- Grilled Avocado with Eggs
- Breakfast Pizza with Bacon and Eggs
- Chicken Salad Croissants
- Fruit Salad with Honey-Lime Dressing
- Ricotta and Spinach Stuffed Crepes
- Egg and Sausage Breakfast Casserole
- Churros with Cinnamon Sugar
- Savory Oatmeal with Poached Egg
- Sweet Potato and Kale Salad
- Avocado and Bacon Breakfast Skillet
- Fluffy Scrambled Eggs with Herbs
- Carrot Cake Pancakes

Classic Eggs Benedict

Ingredients:

- 2 English muffins, split
- 4 slices Canadian bacon
- 4 large eggs
- 1 tablespoon white vinegar
- 1/2 cup hollandaise sauce (store-bought or homemade)
- Fresh parsley, chopped (for garnish)

Instructions:

1. Toast the English muffin halves and set aside.
2. In a skillet, cook the Canadian bacon until lightly browned. Place one slice on each muffin half.
3. In a pot of simmering water with vinegar, carefully poach the eggs for 3-4 minutes until the whites are set.
4. Place a poached egg on top of each muffin and bacon slice.
5. Spoon hollandaise sauce over the eggs and garnish with parsley. Serve immediately.

Avocado Toast with Poached Egg

Ingredients:

- 2 slices whole grain or sourdough bread, toasted
- 1 ripe avocado, mashed
- 2 large eggs
- 1 tablespoon vinegar (for poaching eggs)
- Salt and pepper to taste
- Red pepper flakes (optional)

Instructions:

1. Mash the avocado and spread it over the toasted bread.
2. In a pot of simmering water with vinegar, poach the eggs for about 3-4 minutes.
3. Place a poached egg on top of each avocado toast.
4. Sprinkle with salt, pepper, and red pepper flakes if desired. Serve immediately.

French Toast Casserole

Ingredients:

- 1 loaf challah or brioche, cubed
- 6 large eggs
- 1 1/2 cups milk
- 1 teaspoon vanilla extract
- 1/2 teaspoon cinnamon
- 1/4 cup maple syrup
- Powdered sugar (for dusting)
- Fresh berries (optional)

Instructions:

1. Preheat the oven to 350°F (175°C). Grease a 9x13-inch baking dish.
2. Arrange the cubed bread in the dish.
3. In a bowl, whisk together eggs, milk, vanilla, cinnamon, and maple syrup. Pour this mixture over the bread cubes.
4. Bake for 35-40 minutes or until golden brown and set.
5. Dust with powdered sugar and serve with fresh berries.

Spinach and Feta Quiche

Ingredients:

- 1 pre-made pie crust
- 2 cups fresh spinach, chopped
- 1/2 cup feta cheese, crumbled
- 1/2 cup heavy cream
- 4 large eggs
- 1/4 cup grated Parmesan cheese
- Salt and pepper to taste

Instructions:

1. Preheat the oven to 375°F (190°C).
2. In a skillet, sauté spinach until wilted. Let cool.
3. In a bowl, whisk together eggs, cream, Parmesan, salt, and pepper.
4. Layer the spinach and feta in the pie crust, then pour the egg mixture over it.
5. Bake for 30-35 minutes or until the center is set. Serve warm.

Smoked Salmon Bagels

Ingredients:

- 2 bagels, sliced
- 4 ounces smoked salmon
- 4 ounces cream cheese
- 1 small red onion, thinly sliced
- Capers (optional)
- Fresh dill for garnish

Instructions:

1. Toast the bagel halves.
2. Spread cream cheese on each half.
3. Top with smoked salmon, red onion, capers, and dill. Serve immediately.

Banana Pancakes with Maple Syrup

Ingredients:

- 1 cup all-purpose flour
- 1 tablespoon sugar
- 1 teaspoon baking powder
- 1/2 teaspoon baking soda
- 1/2 teaspoon salt
- 1 egg
- 1 cup buttermilk
- 1 ripe banana, mashed
- 2 tablespoons melted butter
- Maple syrup (for serving)

Instructions:

1. In a bowl, whisk together the dry ingredients.
2. In a separate bowl, mix the egg, buttermilk, mashed banana, and melted butter.
3. Pour the wet ingredients into the dry ingredients and stir until combined.
4. Heat a griddle over medium heat and cook pancakes until bubbles form on the surface. Flip and cook until golden brown.
5. Serve with maple syrup.

Shakshuka (Poached Eggs in Tomato Sauce)

Ingredients:

- 1 tablespoon olive oil
- 1 onion, diced
- 1 bell pepper, diced
- 2 garlic cloves, minced
- 1 can (14 oz) diced tomatoes
- 1 teaspoon cumin
- 1 teaspoon paprika
- 1/2 teaspoon chili flakes
- 4 large eggs
- Fresh cilantro for garnish

Instructions:

1. Heat olive oil in a skillet over medium heat. Add onion and bell pepper, sautéing until soft.
2. Add garlic and cook for 1 minute.
3. Add diced tomatoes, cumin, paprika, and chili flakes. Simmer for 10-15 minutes until the sauce thickens.
4. Make wells in the sauce and crack the eggs into them. Cover and cook for 5-7 minutes or until eggs are cooked to your liking.
5. Garnish with cilantro and serve.

Breakfast Burritos

Ingredients:

- 4 large flour tortillas
- 4 large eggs, scrambled
- 1/2 cup cooked breakfast sausage or bacon
- 1/4 cup shredded cheddar cheese
- 1/4 cup salsa
- 1/4 cup sour cream

Instructions:

1. Heat the tortillas in a skillet until warm.
2. Place scrambled eggs, sausage, cheese, salsa, and sour cream in the center of each tortilla.
3. Fold the sides and roll up the tortillas to form burritos. Serve immediately.

Brioche French Toast

Ingredients:

- 4 slices brioche bread
- 2 large eggs
- 1/2 cup milk
- 1/2 teaspoon cinnamon
- 1/4 teaspoon vanilla extract
- 1 tablespoon butter
- Powdered sugar (for dusting)
- Maple syrup (for serving)

Instructions:

1. In a bowl, whisk together eggs, milk, cinnamon, and vanilla.
2. Heat a skillet over medium heat and melt butter.
3. Dip the brioche slices into the egg mixture, coating both sides, and cook in the skillet until golden brown on both sides.
4. Dust with powdered sugar and serve with maple syrup.

Veggie Omelette with Goat Cheese

Ingredients:

- 3 large eggs
- 1/4 cup milk
- 1/2 bell pepper, diced
- 1/4 onion, diced
- 1/2 cup spinach, chopped
- 1/4 cup mushrooms, sliced
- 2 tablespoons goat cheese, crumbled
- Salt and pepper to taste
- Olive oil for cooking

Instructions:

1. Whisk the eggs with milk, salt, and pepper.
2. Heat a skillet with a little olive oil. Add the bell pepper, onion, spinach, and mushrooms, cooking until softened.
3. Pour the egg mixture into the skillet and let it cook for about 1-2 minutes until the edges set.
4. Sprinkle the goat cheese on one half of the omelette and fold it over. Cook for another minute until the cheese is melted.
5. Serve warm.

Spinach and Mushroom Frittata

Ingredients:

- 8 large eggs
- 1/2 cup heavy cream
- 1 cup spinach, chopped
- 1/2 cup mushrooms, sliced
- 1/2 onion, diced
- 1/4 cup feta cheese, crumbled
- Olive oil for cooking
- Salt and pepper to taste

Instructions:

1. Preheat the oven to 375°F (190°C).
2. Heat olive oil in a skillet over medium heat and sauté onions, mushrooms, and spinach until softened.
3. In a bowl, whisk together eggs, heavy cream, salt, and pepper. Pour the egg mixture over the sautéed vegetables in the skillet.
4. Sprinkle feta cheese on top and transfer the skillet to the oven. Bake for 15-20 minutes or until the eggs are set.
5. Slice and serve.

Sweet Potato Hash

Ingredients:

- 2 medium sweet potatoes, peeled and diced
- 1 red bell pepper, diced
- 1/2 onion, diced
- 1 tablespoon olive oil
- 1 teaspoon paprika
- Salt and pepper to taste
- 2 large eggs (optional, for topping)

Instructions:

1. Heat olive oil in a skillet over medium heat. Add the sweet potatoes and cook for 8-10 minutes until they start to soften.
2. Add the bell pepper, onion, paprika, salt, and pepper. Continue cooking for another 5-7 minutes until everything is tender and lightly browned.
3. Optional: Fry the eggs in a separate pan and place them on top of the hash for serving.
4. Serve warm and enjoy.

Lemon Ricotta Pancakes

Ingredients:

- 1 cup all-purpose flour
- 1 tablespoon sugar
- 1 teaspoon baking powder
- 1/2 teaspoon baking soda
- 1/4 teaspoon salt
- 1 cup ricotta cheese
- 1 large egg
- 1/2 cup milk
- Zest of 1 lemon
- 1 tablespoon lemon juice
- Butter for cooking

Instructions:

1. In a bowl, whisk together the dry ingredients.
2. In another bowl, combine ricotta, egg, milk, lemon zest, and lemon juice.
3. Pour the wet ingredients into the dry ingredients and stir until just combined.
4. Heat a skillet over medium heat and melt butter. Pour 1/4 cup of batter onto the skillet for each pancake and cook until bubbles form. Flip and cook until golden brown on both sides.
5. Serve with syrup or fresh fruit.

Egg and Avocado Breakfast Sandwich

Ingredients:

- 2 slices whole grain bread, toasted
- 2 large eggs
- 1/2 avocado, sliced
- 1 tablespoon mayonnaise or mustard (optional)
- Salt and pepper to taste
- Fresh spinach leaves (optional)

Instructions:

1. Fry the eggs in a skillet to your desired doneness.
2. Toast the bread and spread mayonnaise or mustard if using.
3. Place a fried egg on one slice of toast, then top with avocado slices, spinach, salt, and pepper.
4. Place the other slice of bread on top and serve.

Croissant Breakfast Sandwich

Ingredients:

- 2 buttery croissants, sliced in half
- 2 large eggs
- 2 slices cheddar cheese
- 2 slices cooked bacon or sausage patty
- Fresh spinach or arugula (optional)

Instructions:

1. Fry the eggs to your preferred doneness.
2. Split the croissants in half and warm them in the oven or on a skillet.
3. Layer the eggs, cheese, bacon, and spinach on one half of the croissant. Top with the other half.
4. Serve warm.

Chia Pudding with Mixed Berries

Ingredients:

- 1/4 cup chia seeds
- 1 cup almond milk or milk of choice
- 1 tablespoon honey or maple syrup
- 1/2 teaspoon vanilla extract
- 1/2 cup mixed berries (strawberries, blueberries, raspberries)

Instructions:

1. In a bowl, combine chia seeds, milk, honey, and vanilla extract. Stir well.
2. Cover and refrigerate for at least 4 hours or overnight, allowing the chia seeds to absorb the liquid and thicken.
3. Top with fresh mixed berries before serving.

Buttermilk Waffles with Whipped Cream

Ingredients:

- 2 cups all-purpose flour
- 2 tablespoons sugar
- 1 tablespoon baking powder
- 1/2 teaspoon salt
- 2 large eggs
- 1 3/4 cups buttermilk
- 1/4 cup unsalted butter, melted
- 1 teaspoon vanilla extract
- Whipped cream (for topping)

Instructions:

1. Preheat your waffle iron.
2. In a large bowl, whisk together the flour, sugar, baking powder, and salt.
3. In a separate bowl, beat the eggs and mix with buttermilk, melted butter, and vanilla extract.
4. Pour the wet ingredients into the dry ingredients and stir until just combined.
5. Cook the waffles according to your waffle iron's instructions.
6. Serve with whipped cream and syrup.

Roasted Tomato and Herb Salad

Ingredients:

- 2 cups cherry or grape tomatoes, halved
- 1 tablespoon olive oil
- Salt and pepper to taste
- 1/4 cup fresh basil leaves, chopped
- 1/4 cup fresh parsley, chopped
- 1 tablespoon balsamic vinegar

Instructions:

1. Preheat the oven to 400°F (200°C).
2. Toss the halved tomatoes with olive oil, salt, and pepper, then spread them on a baking sheet.
3. Roast for 15-20 minutes or until the tomatoes are softened and slightly caramelized.
4. Toss with fresh basil, parsley, and balsamic vinegar.
5. Serve warm or at room temperature.

Blueberry Muffins

Ingredients:

- 1 1/2 cups all-purpose flour
- 1 teaspoon baking powder
- 1/2 teaspoon baking soda
- 1/2 teaspoon salt
- 1/2 cup unsalted butter, softened
- 3/4 cup sugar
- 2 large eggs
- 1 teaspoon vanilla extract
- 1/2 cup buttermilk
- 1 1/2 cups fresh blueberries

Instructions:

1. Preheat the oven to 350°F (175°C) and line a muffin tin with paper liners.
2. In a bowl, whisk together flour, baking powder, baking soda, and salt.
3. In a separate bowl, beat the butter and sugar until light and fluffy. Add the eggs one at a time, mixing well after each addition.
4. Stir in the vanilla extract, then alternately add the dry ingredients and buttermilk to the butter mixture, starting and ending with the dry ingredients.
5. Gently fold in the blueberries.
6. Spoon the batter into the muffin tin and bake for 20-25 minutes or until a toothpick comes out clean.
7. Allow to cool before serving.

Baked Eggs with Spinach and Bacon

Ingredients:

- 4 large eggs
- 1 cup fresh spinach, chopped
- 2 slices bacon, cooked and crumbled
- 1/4 cup grated Parmesan cheese
- Salt and pepper to taste
- Olive oil for greasing

Instructions:

1. Preheat the oven to 375°F (190°C) and grease a small baking dish.
2. In a pan, sauté the spinach with a little olive oil until wilted.
3. In the greased baking dish, layer the sautéed spinach and crumbled bacon.
4. Crack the eggs on top and season with salt and pepper.
5. Sprinkle Parmesan cheese on top and bake for 10-12 minutes, or until the eggs are cooked to your liking.
6. Serve warm.

Smoothie Bowls with Fresh Toppings

Ingredients:

- 1 frozen banana
- 1/2 cup frozen mixed berries
- 1/2 cup almond milk or milk of choice
- 1 tablespoon chia seeds
- Toppings: sliced fruit, granola, coconut flakes, nuts, or seeds

Instructions:

1. In a blender, combine the banana, berries, almond milk, and chia seeds. Blend until smooth.
2. Pour the smoothie into a bowl.
3. Top with your choice of sliced fruit, granola, coconut flakes, nuts, or seeds.
4. Serve immediately.

Cucumber and Cream Cheese Sandwiches

Ingredients:

- 8 slices white or whole wheat bread
- 1/2 cup cream cheese, softened
- 1/2 cucumber, thinly sliced
- Salt and pepper to taste
- Fresh dill (optional)

Instructions:

1. Spread the cream cheese evenly on each slice of bread.
2. Layer the cucumber slices on top of one slice of bread.
3. Season with salt, pepper, and fresh dill if desired.
4. Top with the other slice of bread to complete the sandwich.
5. Slice into halves or quarters and serve.

Grilled Cheese and Tomato Soup

Ingredients:

- 4 slices bread
- 4 slices cheddar cheese
- 2 tablespoons butter
- 2 cups tomato soup (store-bought or homemade)

Instructions:

1. Preheat a skillet over medium heat and butter one side of each slice of bread.
2. Place a slice of cheese between two slices of bread, buttered sides out.
3. Grill the sandwich in the skillet until golden brown on both sides and the cheese is melted, about 3-4 minutes per side.
4. Heat the tomato soup in a pot over medium heat until warm.
5. Serve the grilled cheese with the tomato soup for dipping.

Chicken and Waffle Sliders

Ingredients:

- 4 mini waffles
- 2 fried chicken tenders
- Maple syrup
- Butter for cooking

Instructions:

1. Toast the mini waffles according to package instructions.
2. Cook or heat the fried chicken tenders.
3. Assemble the sliders by placing a chicken tender between two waffles.
4. Drizzle with maple syrup and add a little butter on top for extra flavor.
5. Serve warm.

Smashed Avocado and Toast with Poached Eggs

Ingredients:

- 2 slices whole grain bread
- 1 ripe avocado
- 2 large eggs
- 1 tablespoon olive oil
- Salt and pepper to taste

Instructions:

1. Toast the slices of bread until golden brown.
2. Mash the avocado with a fork, adding salt, pepper, and olive oil.
3. Poach the eggs by simmering water in a pan, cracking the eggs into the water, and cooking for about 4 minutes until the whites are set.
4. Spread the mashed avocado on the toast and top with poached eggs.
5. Serve immediately.

Greek Yogurt Parfait with Granola

Ingredients:

- 1 cup Greek yogurt
- 1/2 cup granola
- 1/2 cup fresh berries (strawberries, blueberries, raspberries)
- Honey (optional)

Instructions:

1. In a glass or bowl, layer Greek yogurt, granola, and fresh berries.
2. Drizzle with honey if desired for extra sweetness.
3. Serve immediately or refrigerate for later.

Sweet Corn Fritters

Ingredients:

- 2 cups fresh corn kernels (or frozen, thawed)
- 1 cup all-purpose flour
- 1/2 teaspoon baking powder
- 1/4 teaspoon salt
- 1/4 teaspoon black pepper
- 1/2 teaspoon paprika
- 1/4 cup milk
- 2 large eggs
- 1 tablespoon chopped fresh parsley (optional)
- Oil for frying

Instructions:

1. In a bowl, combine the corn, flour, baking powder, salt, pepper, and paprika.
2. In another bowl, whisk together the milk and eggs, then pour into the dry ingredients and stir until just combined.
3. Heat oil in a skillet over medium heat.
4. Drop spoonfuls of the batter into the skillet and flatten slightly with the back of the spoon. Fry until golden brown on both sides, about 3 minutes per side.
5. Remove from the skillet and drain on paper towels.
6. Serve warm with a dollop of sour cream or your favorite dipping sauce.

Salmon Croquettes with Dill Sauce

Ingredients:

For the croquettes:

- 1 can (14.75 oz) pink salmon, drained and flaked
- 1/2 cup breadcrumbs
- 1/4 cup finely chopped onion
- 1/4 cup finely chopped bell pepper
- 1 tablespoon mayonnaise
- 1 tablespoon Dijon mustard
- 1 egg
- Salt and pepper to taste
- Oil for frying

For the dill sauce:

- 1/2 cup sour cream
- 1 tablespoon mayonnaise
- 1 tablespoon fresh dill, chopped
- 1 teaspoon lemon juice
- Salt and pepper to taste

Instructions:

1. In a bowl, combine the salmon, breadcrumbs, onion, bell pepper, mayonnaise, mustard, egg, salt, and pepper.
2. Form the mixture into small patties.
3. Heat oil in a skillet over medium heat and fry the croquettes for 3-4 minutes per side until golden and crispy.
4. For the dill sauce, combine the sour cream, mayonnaise, dill, lemon juice, salt, and pepper in a small bowl.
5. Serve the croquettes with a generous dollop of dill sauce.

Mimosas with Fresh Orange Juice

Ingredients:

- 1 bottle champagne or sparkling wine
- 1 cup fresh orange juice
- Orange slices for garnish

Instructions:

1. Pour fresh orange juice into a champagne flute, filling it about one-third full.
2. Slowly top with chilled champagne or sparkling wine.
3. Garnish with a slice of orange on the rim of the glass.
4. Serve immediately and enjoy!

Sourdough Pancakes

Ingredients:

- 1 cup sourdough starter (fed or unfed)
- 1/2 cup milk
- 1 tablespoon sugar
- 1 large egg
- 2 tablespoons melted butter
- 1/2 teaspoon vanilla extract
- 1/2 teaspoon baking soda
- Pinch of salt

Instructions:

1. In a bowl, whisk together the sourdough starter, milk, sugar, egg, butter, and vanilla extract.
2. In another bowl, mix the baking soda and salt, then add it to the wet ingredients. Stir until smooth.
3. Heat a griddle or skillet over medium heat and lightly grease it.
4. Pour batter onto the griddle, using about 1/4 cup for each pancake.
5. Cook until bubbles form on the surface, then flip and cook until golden brown on both sides.
6. Serve with maple syrup and your favorite toppings.

Caprese Salad with Fresh Mozzarella

Ingredients:

- 3 large tomatoes, sliced
- 8 oz fresh mozzarella cheese, sliced
- 1/4 cup fresh basil leaves
- 2 tablespoons extra-virgin olive oil
- 1 tablespoon balsamic vinegar
- Salt and pepper to taste

Instructions:

1. Arrange the sliced tomatoes and mozzarella on a platter, alternating between the two.
2. Tuck the fresh basil leaves between the slices of tomato and mozzarella.
3. Drizzle with olive oil and balsamic vinegar.
4. Season with salt and pepper.
5. Serve immediately as a refreshing appetizer or side dish.

Zucchini Fritters with Lemon Aioli

Ingredients:

For the fritters:

- 2 medium zucchinis, grated
- 1/2 teaspoon salt
- 1/2 cup all-purpose flour
- 1/4 cup grated Parmesan cheese
- 1 egg, beaten
- 1 clove garlic, minced
- 1 tablespoon chopped fresh parsley
- Oil for frying

For the lemon aioli:

- 1/2 cup mayonnaise
- 1 tablespoon lemon juice
- 1 teaspoon Dijon mustard
- 1 garlic clove, minced
- Salt and pepper to taste

Instructions:

1. Sprinkle the grated zucchini with salt and let sit for 10 minutes.
2. Squeeze out the excess moisture from the zucchini.
3. In a bowl, combine the zucchini, flour, Parmesan, egg, garlic, parsley, salt, and pepper.
4. Heat oil in a skillet over medium heat. Drop spoonfuls of the mixture into the pan and flatten into patties. Fry for 2-3 minutes per side, until golden and crispy.
5. For the aioli, combine mayonnaise, lemon juice, Dijon mustard, garlic, salt, and pepper in a bowl.
6. Serve the fritters warm with the lemon aioli.

Breakfast Tacos with Salsa Verde

Ingredients:

- 4 small soft tortillas
- 4 eggs
- 1/2 cup cooked breakfast sausage or bacon, crumbled
- 1/4 cup shredded cheese (cheddar or Mexican blend)
- Salsa verde
- Fresh cilantro for garnish

Instructions:

1. Scramble the eggs in a skillet over medium heat until cooked to your liking.
2. Warm the tortillas in a dry pan or microwave.
3. Assemble the tacos by spooning scrambled eggs onto each tortilla, followed by sausage or bacon, cheese, and salsa verde.
4. Garnish with fresh cilantro and serve immediately.

Roasted Vegetable Tart

Ingredients:

- 1 sheet puff pastry
- 1 cup mixed roasted vegetables (such as bell peppers, zucchini, and onions)
- 1/2 cup goat cheese or cream cheese
- 1 tablespoon olive oil
- Salt and pepper to taste
- Fresh thyme for garnish

Instructions:

1. Preheat the oven to 375°F (190°C).
2. Roll out the puff pastry on a baking sheet lined with parchment paper.
3. Spread a thin layer of goat cheese or cream cheese on the pastry, leaving a border around the edges.
4. Top with the roasted vegetables and drizzle with olive oil.
5. Season with salt and pepper, then fold the edges of the pastry over the vegetables to create a rustic tart.
6. Bake for 20-25 minutes, until the pastry is golden and crisp.
7. Garnish with fresh thyme and serve warm.

Bacon, Egg, and Cheese Croissant

Ingredients:

- 2 large croissants
- 4 slices cooked bacon
- 2 large eggs
- 2 slices cheddar cheese
- 1 tablespoon butter
- Salt and pepper to taste

Instructions:

1. Cut the croissants in half horizontally and lightly toast them in a toaster or oven.
2. In a skillet, melt the butter over medium heat and cook the eggs to your liking (scrambled or fried). Season with salt and pepper.
3. Place a slice of cheese on top of the eggs to melt slightly.
4. Layer the eggs, bacon, and the other half of the croissant together.
5. Serve warm and enjoy!

Stuffed Bell Peppers with Quinoa and Eggs

Ingredients:

- 4 bell peppers, tops cut off and seeds removed
- 1 cup cooked quinoa
- 1/2 cup black beans, drained and rinsed
- 1/2 cup corn kernels
- 1/2 cup shredded cheese (cheddar or Mexican blend)
- 4 large eggs
- 1 tablespoon olive oil
- Salt and pepper to taste
- Fresh cilantro for garnish

Instructions:

1. Preheat the oven to 375°F (190°C).
2. In a bowl, combine the cooked quinoa, black beans, corn, cheese, salt, and pepper.
3. Stuff each bell pepper with the quinoa mixture and place them in a baking dish.
4. Create a small well in the center of each stuffed pepper and crack an egg into the well.
5. Drizzle the peppers with olive oil and bake for 20-25 minutes, until the eggs are set to your liking.
6. Garnish with fresh cilantro and serve warm.

Lemon Poppy Seed Muffins

Ingredients:

- 1 1/2 cups all-purpose flour
- 1 teaspoon baking powder
- 1/2 teaspoon baking soda
- 1/4 teaspoon salt
- 2 tablespoons poppy seeds
- 1/2 cup sugar
- 2 large eggs
- 1/2 cup milk
- 1/4 cup vegetable oil
- 1 teaspoon vanilla extract
- Zest of 1 lemon
- 2 tablespoons fresh lemon juice

Instructions:

1. Preheat the oven to 375°F (190°C) and line a muffin tin with paper liners.
2. In a bowl, whisk together the flour, baking powder, baking soda, salt, and poppy seeds.
3. In another bowl, beat the eggs and mix in the sugar, milk, oil, vanilla extract, lemon zest, and lemon juice.
4. Gradually add the wet ingredients to the dry ingredients and stir until just combined.
5. Fill the muffin cups about 2/3 full with batter.
6. Bake for 18-20 minutes, until a toothpick comes out clean.
7. Let cool in the tin for 5 minutes before transferring to a wire rack.

Quinoa Salad with Roasted Veggies

Ingredients:

- 1 cup cooked quinoa
- 1 zucchini, diced
- 1 red bell pepper, diced
- 1 small red onion, diced
- 1 tablespoon olive oil
- 1 teaspoon dried oregano
- Salt and pepper to taste
- 1/4 cup crumbled feta cheese
- Fresh parsley for garnish
- Lemon vinaigrette dressing

Instructions:

1. Preheat the oven to 400°F (200°C).
2. Toss the zucchini, bell pepper, and onion with olive oil, oregano, salt, and pepper.
3. Spread the vegetables on a baking sheet and roast for 20-25 minutes, until tender.
4. In a large bowl, combine the cooked quinoa and roasted vegetables.
5. Toss in the crumbled feta cheese and garnish with fresh parsley.
6. Drizzle with lemon vinaigrette dressing before serving.

Grilled Avocado with Eggs

Ingredients:

- 2 ripe avocados, halved and pitted
- 2 eggs
- 1 tablespoon olive oil
- Salt and pepper to taste
- Hot sauce (optional)
- Fresh cilantro for garnish

Instructions:

1. Preheat the grill or grill pan to medium heat.
2. Drizzle the avocado halves with olive oil and season with salt and pepper.
3. Place the avocado halves on the grill, flesh side down, and cook for 2-3 minutes, until grill marks appear.
4. While the avocados are grilling, cook the eggs to your liking in a separate skillet.
5. Place a cooked egg in the center of each avocado half.
6. Serve immediately with hot sauce and fresh cilantro.

Breakfast Pizza with Bacon and Eggs

Ingredients:

- 1 pizza dough (store-bought or homemade)
- 4 slices cooked bacon, crumbled
- 2 eggs
- 1/2 cup shredded mozzarella cheese
- 1/4 cup grated Parmesan cheese
- 1 tablespoon olive oil
- Salt and pepper to taste
- Fresh basil for garnish

Instructions:

1. Preheat the oven to 475°F (245°C).
2. Roll out the pizza dough on a baking sheet or pizza stone.
3. Brush the dough with olive oil and sprinkle with mozzarella cheese and Parmesan.
4. Bake for 8-10 minutes, until the crust is golden.
5. Crack the eggs onto the pizza and sprinkle with bacon, salt, and pepper.
6. Return to the oven and bake for another 5-7 minutes, until the eggs are cooked to your liking.
7. Garnish with fresh basil and serve immediately.

Chicken Salad Croissants

Ingredients:

- 2 cups cooked chicken, shredded
- 1/2 cup mayonnaise
- 1 tablespoon Dijon mustard
- 1 tablespoon lemon juice
- 1/4 cup chopped celery
- 1/4 cup chopped red grapes
- Salt and pepper to taste
- 4 croissants, halved

Instructions:

1. In a bowl, combine the shredded chicken, mayonnaise, Dijon mustard, lemon juice, celery, and grapes.
2. Season with salt and pepper to taste.
3. Spoon the chicken salad onto the bottom half of the croissants.
4. Top with the other half of the croissant and serve immediately.

Fruit Salad with Honey-Lime Dressing

Ingredients:

- 2 cups mixed fresh fruit (such as strawberries, pineapple, mango, and blueberries)
- 1 tablespoon honey
- 1 tablespoon fresh lime juice
- 1/2 teaspoon lime zest
- Fresh mint leaves for garnish

Instructions:

1. In a bowl, combine the fresh fruit.
2. In a small bowl, whisk together the honey, lime juice, and lime zest.
3. Drizzle the honey-lime dressing over the fruit and toss gently.
4. Garnish with fresh mint leaves and serve chilled.

Ricotta and Spinach Stuffed Crepes

Ingredients:

For the crepes:

- 1 cup all-purpose flour
- 1 cup milk
- 2 large eggs
- 2 tablespoons melted butter
- Pinch of salt

For the filling:

- 1 cup ricotta cheese
- 1/2 cup cooked spinach, squeezed dry
- 1/4 cup grated Parmesan cheese
- Salt and pepper to taste

Instructions:

1. In a bowl, whisk together the flour, milk, eggs, melted butter, and salt until smooth.
2. Heat a non-stick skillet over medium heat and pour in a small amount of batter, swirling to coat the bottom of the pan.
3. Cook for 1-2 minutes, then flip and cook for another 1 minute. Remove and set aside.
4. In a separate bowl, mix the ricotta, cooked spinach, Parmesan, salt, and pepper.
5. Spoon the ricotta mixture onto each crepe and roll them up.
6. Serve warm, optionally garnished with extra Parmesan.

Egg and Sausage Breakfast Casserole

Ingredients:

- 1 lb breakfast sausage, cooked and crumbled
- 6 large eggs
- 1 1/2 cups milk
- 1 1/2 cups shredded cheese (cheddar or a mix)
- 1/2 cup diced onion
- 1/2 cup diced bell pepper
- 2 cups cubed bread (preferably day-old or slightly toasted)
- Salt and pepper to taste
- 1/2 teaspoon garlic powder
- 1/2 teaspoon dried oregano

Instructions:

1. Preheat the oven to 350°F (175°C).
2. In a large bowl, whisk together the eggs, milk, salt, pepper, garlic powder, and oregano.
3. Add the cooked sausage, diced onion, diced bell pepper, and cubed bread to the egg mixture and stir to combine.
4. Pour the mixture into a greased 9x13-inch baking dish and top with shredded cheese.
5. Bake for 35-40 minutes, or until the casserole is set and the top is golden.
6. Let cool for a few minutes before slicing and serving.

Churros with Cinnamon Sugar

Ingredients:

- 1 cup water
- 2 tablespoons butter
- 1 tablespoon sugar
- 1/2 teaspoon vanilla extract
- 1 cup all-purpose flour
- 1/4 teaspoon salt
- 2 large eggs
- Oil for frying
- 1/2 cup sugar (for coating)
- 1 teaspoon ground cinnamon

Instructions:

1. In a saucepan, combine water, butter, sugar, and vanilla extract. Heat until the butter is melted and the mixture comes to a simmer.
2. Stir in the flour and salt until the mixture forms a dough. Continue to cook for 1-2 minutes, stirring constantly.
3. Remove from heat and let cool slightly. Stir in the eggs, one at a time, until the dough is smooth.
4. Heat oil in a deep skillet or pot to 350°F (175°C).
5. Transfer the dough to a piping bag fitted with a star tip.
6. Pipe 3-4 inch strips of dough into the hot oil, frying in batches for 2-3 minutes, or until golden brown.
7. Remove from oil and drain on paper towels.
8. In a bowl, mix sugar and cinnamon. Roll the churros in the cinnamon sugar mixture while still warm.
9. Serve immediately with chocolate sauce or a dipping sauce of your choice.

Savory Oatmeal with Poached Egg

Ingredients:

- 1 cup old-fashioned oats
- 2 cups chicken or vegetable broth
- 1/2 teaspoon salt
- Freshly ground black pepper to taste
- 1 tablespoon olive oil
- 1/4 cup grated cheese (cheddar, parmesan, or your choice)
- 2 large eggs
- Fresh herbs for garnish (such as parsley or chives)

Instructions:

1. In a saucepan, bring the chicken or vegetable broth to a simmer.
2. Stir in the oats and salt, and cook over medium heat for about 5-7 minutes, until the oats are tender and the mixture thickens.
3. Stir in olive oil and grated cheese until melted and creamy. Adjust seasoning with pepper.
4. While the oats cook, bring a pot of water to a simmer and poach the eggs for about 3-4 minutes until the whites are set but the yolk is still runny.
5. Spoon the savory oatmeal into bowls and top with a poached egg. Garnish with fresh herbs and serve warm.

Sweet Potato and Kale Salad

Ingredients:

- 2 medium sweet potatoes, peeled and diced
- 2 tablespoons olive oil
- Salt and pepper to taste
- 4 cups chopped kale, stems removed
- 1/4 cup red onion, thinly sliced
- 1/4 cup dried cranberries
- 1/4 cup chopped nuts (walnuts or pecans)
- 1 tablespoon olive oil (for dressing)
- 1 tablespoon balsamic vinegar
- 1 teaspoon honey

Instructions:

1. Preheat the oven to 400°F (200°C).
2. Toss the diced sweet potatoes with olive oil, salt, and pepper, then spread them on a baking sheet.
3. Roast for 20-25 minutes, or until the sweet potatoes are tender and lightly browned.
4. In a small bowl, whisk together the olive oil, balsamic vinegar, and honey to make the dressing.
5. In a large bowl, combine the chopped kale, red onion, cranberries, and nuts.
6. Add the roasted sweet potatoes to the salad and toss everything together with the dressing.
7. Serve immediately, or refrigerate for later.

Avocado and Bacon Breakfast Skillet

Ingredients:

- 4 slices bacon
- 1 large avocado, sliced
- 2 large eggs
- 1/4 teaspoon paprika
- Salt and pepper to taste
- Fresh cilantro for garnish

Instructions:

1. In a skillet, cook the bacon over medium heat until crispy. Remove from the skillet and set aside on paper towels to drain.
2. In the same skillet, crack the eggs and cook to your liking (sunny-side-up or scrambled).
3. While the eggs are cooking, slice the avocado and set aside.
4. Once the eggs are done, top them with avocado slices, crispy bacon, paprika, salt, and pepper.
5. Garnish with fresh cilantro and serve immediately.

Fluffy Scrambled Eggs with Herbs

Ingredients:

- 4 large eggs
- 1 tablespoon butter
- 1 tablespoon milk or cream
- Salt and pepper to taste
- Fresh herbs (parsley, chives, or tarragon) for garnish

Instructions:

1. Crack the eggs into a bowl and whisk them together with the milk or cream, salt, and pepper.
2. Heat a skillet over medium-low heat and melt the butter.
3. Pour the egg mixture into the skillet and cook slowly, stirring constantly to prevent them from overcooking.
4. Once the eggs are soft and fluffy, remove from the heat and garnish with fresh herbs.
5. Serve immediately.

Carrot Cake Pancakes

Ingredients:

- 1 1/2 cups all-purpose flour
- 1 teaspoon baking powder
- 1/2 teaspoon baking soda
- 1/2 teaspoon cinnamon
- 1/4 teaspoon nutmeg
- 1/4 teaspoon salt
- 1/2 cup grated carrots
- 1/4 cup milk
- 2 large eggs
- 1/4 cup brown sugar
- 1 teaspoon vanilla extract
- 2 tablespoons butter, melted
- Cream cheese frosting for topping

Instructions:

1. In a bowl, whisk together the flour, baking powder, baking soda, cinnamon, nutmeg, and salt.
2. In another bowl, beat the eggs and mix in the milk, brown sugar, vanilla extract, and melted butter.
3. Stir the wet ingredients into the dry ingredients until just combined.
4. Gently fold in the grated carrots.
5. Heat a non-stick skillet over medium heat and lightly grease it with butter or oil.
6. Pour 1/4 cup of batter onto the skillet for each pancake. Cook for 2-3 minutes on each side, until golden brown.
7. Serve the pancakes warm with a dollop of cream cheese frosting on top.

www.ingramcontent.com/pod-product-compliance
Lightning Source LLC
LaVergne TN
LVHW081334060526
838201LV00055B/2632